SELF ESTEEM

Walking Tall

LEAP Learning Empowerment & Achieving Potential

ISBN 978-93-81115-70-1

First published in 2011 by Leadstart
A brand of One Point Six Technologies Private Limited
Unit no. 26, Ground Floor, A1, Shram Safalya,
Wadala Truck Terminal Road, Near Post Office,
Antop Hill, Mumbai -400037.
Email:info@leadstartcorp.com
www.leadstartcorp.com

Marketed & Distributed in India by Unbound Script
2/41, Ansari Road, Darayaganj, Delhi - 110002

EDITORS OF LEADSTART

The Editors of Leadstart are a team of passionate literary enthusiasts with a creative and progressive focus. Our team includes distinguished authors, researchers, contributors, in-house editors, and writing talent from around the world. Many literary projects require a diverse team rather than a single author to write or update the book. These projects often involve cases where the original author is unable to continue, whether because they are unavailable or no longer with us. Our work thus spans a range of content, from original writings to thoughtfully abridged classics, updated editions, and translations.

ABOUT THE LEAP SERIES

The LEAP series of books has been conceived as a tool of empowerment for every individual to achieve their full potential.

There are certain aspirations that every person in the world shares. We all want to be happy. We all want to lead fulfilling lives. We all want to find our soulmate. We all want a job we love doing. We all want good friends who will share our joy and sorrow. We all want to believe that there is a purpose to our lives.

While the commonality of these goals spans the globe, their achievement is entirely individual. Each person possesses a unique and mixed gift of strengths and weaknesses, special talents and handicaps. To focus our individual lives on all that is positive within us, all that is possible for us to do, to be and to achieve, we need to take conscious steps towards it. The empowerment of our lives is an individual pursuit. The decisions are yours. The action is yours. To do the very best with what one has been given – that is the ultimate achievement of a life well lived.

You Are You
First, we must recognise ourselves and accept our particular basket of capabilities. Nobody is the same. Nor is it necessary to be like someone else.

Find Your Horizons
Once we are at peace with the composition of our own individuality, we can set out to enhance our capabilities in order to achieve full potential as an individual. We can utilise all the teaching around us to stretch our talents to the fullest extent to achieve worthwhile goals.

Cap The Leak
Once we recognise our potential, we can work to minimise the influence and impact of our weak points to allow the strengths to shine in everything we do.

Row Your Boat
Every day is part of the journey. Sometimes you win the day. Sometimes the day is lost. But you keep rowing towards the shore, towards your goals. In India, it is called sadhana. That special power within you drives you to achieve what you have set yourself to do.

The LEAP series teaches methods of individual empowerment.

ƐↄϲϨ

CONTENTS

INTRODUCTION

Every day begins with a conversation, though most people never notice it. It is the one that happens inside your own mind before you have even spoken to anyone else. Before you check your phone, before you meet the world, your thoughts have already begun shaping how you will carry yourself through the day. You might tell yourself that you are ready and capable, or you might begin with hesitation, doubt, or self-criticism. That inner dialogue is not random. It is the voice of your self-esteem, and whether it speaks softly or loudly, whether it uplifts or undermines, it influences everything you do.

Self-esteem is not a luxury, nor is it an abstract concept meant for philosophers and psychologists. It is the invisible framework that supports how you live, love, and work. It determines how you handle failure, how you receive praise, and how you recover when life tests you. When you have a healthy sense of self-worth, challenges are not proof of your weakness but opportunities to grow. When self-esteem is fragile, even small obstacles can feel like personal defeats. This is why two people can face the same difficulty and emerge from it so differently. Confidence and resilience are not simply traits; they are outcomes of how much value you assign to yourself in your own eyes.

The late broadcaster Larry King once said in an interview that the best advice he could give anyone is to work on their self-esteem. It is a simple truth that many people overlook while chasing success, relationships, and validation. They keep trying to earn a sense of worth from the outside, yet what they are seeking must come from within. Self-esteem cannot be permanently supplied by approval, praise, or love from others. Those things may affirm it, but they cannot build it. The work begins with how you choose to see yourself when no one else is watching.

Low self-esteem does not always look like sadness or shyness. Sometimes it hides behind humour, busyness, or loudness. Some people keep moving constantly, trying to prove their value through achievement or attention, while others withdraw completely, avoiding situations where they might fail or be seen too closely. The form may differ, but the feeling beneath is the same: a conviction that you are somehow not enough. This belief not only limits ambition; it also erodes relationships, creativity, and peace of mind. It can make you over-apologetic or defensive, dependent on approval, or suspicious of kindness. It can convince you that love must be earned through suffering, that mistakes define who you are, or that confidence belongs only to other people.

The song *Self-Esteem* by Offspring captures this painful contradiction vividly. The narrator knows he is being mistreated, yet keeps returning to a relationship that diminishes him. He recognises the manipulation and even mocks himself for tolerating it, but the truth is that he does not believe he deserves better. This is not just a song about romance; it is a song about human psychology. When your sense of worth collapses, even unhappiness begins to feel familiar, and familiarity feels safer than change. This pattern repeats in many lives, in workplaces where people accept unfair treatment, in friendships that only take and never give, and in families where old emotional wounds still hold power. The core issue is not weakness; it is disconnection from one's own value.

Confidence is often misunderstood as perfection, yet it has little to do with flawlessness. True confidence grows from the willingness to face imperfection with respect for oneself. It lives in the assurance that mistakes do not erase worth, that vulnerability is not failure, and that progress is possible without comparison. When you understand that you are already enough as you are, you stop performing for approval and begin to act from authenticity. This shift does not make life easier, but it makes it clearer. It allows you to meet the world on your own terms, not through the distorted lens of insecurity.

The encouraging truth is that self-esteem is not permanent in either direction. It is not something you are born with or without, nor something that fades forever when lost. It is a skill that can be rebuilt at any stage of life. You can begin again, no matter your past. You can learn to replace the voice that criticises with one that guides, to speak to yourself with patience instead of punishment, and to view mistakes as lessons rather than verdicts. This process takes time, but every act of awareness is a step toward strength.

Developing healthy self-esteem is not about inflating the ego or pretending that everything about you is perfect. It is about balance.

It is knowing your strengths without denying your flaws, valuing your individuality without needing to be superior, and recognising that worth is not earned by performance but affirmed by existence. You do not need to become someone else to feel worthy. You need only to meet yourself with honesty and respect. When you do, the confidence that follows is not arrogance but peace.

Everyone carries strengths that have often gone unnoticed. They might be the patience you show in a crisis, the care you give without being asked, or the creativity you hide because you doubt its value. These qualities do not disappear simply because you stopped believing in them; they wait patiently for recognition. When you begin to rebuild your self-esteem, what you are really doing is uncovering what has always been there. It is an excavation, not an invention. You learn to see yourself as whole again, imperfect, evolving, but deeply capable.

This work begins with a decision: the decision to stop living as though your worth depends on other people's treatment or approval. You start by paying attention to your own voice, by questioning the stories you have told yourself about who you are, and by choosing kinder interpretations of your experience. You practice small acts of respect, such as keeping promises to yourself, setting boundaries, or speaking truthfully about how you feel. Over time, these acts become habits, and those habits form the backbone of self-respect.

A person with healthy self-esteem is not someone who never doubts or fails, but someone who knows how to recover without losing themselves in the process. They know how to walk away from what harms them and how to stay grounded in what nourishes them. They can give love without fear of rejection and receive love without suspicion. Their sense of worth is not fragile because it is not borrowed; it is self-made.

This book is a guide to that kind of strength. It will explore how self-esteem forms, how it is influenced by relationships and society, and how it can be rebuilt when damaged. It will look at the unique challenges of different life stages, from childhood to adulthood, and how family, education, culture, and media shape our inner voice. You will find not just reflection, but also tools, ways to practice self-compassion, to encourage confidence in others, and to protect your own peace.

Wherever you are in your journey, remember that self-esteem is not a finish line. It is a relationship you have with yourself that evolves over time. You do not have to fix everything overnight. You only have to begin. Each time you choose respect over criticism, patience over shame, and growth over perfection, you strengthen that relationship.

The path to self-worth begins with a simple truth: you are already enough. The rest of the journey is about learning to believe it again.

ꕥ

1

DEFINING SELF-ESTEEM

Every person carries a mirror in their mind. It is not made of glass or silver, yet it reflects more powerfully than any physical object. This mirror shows not your face, but your worth. It determines how you see yourself, how you speak to yourself, and how you believe others see you. The image you carry within shapes every decision you make, from the risks you take to the dreams you allow yourself to chase. This is self-esteem, the mental and emotional picture that guides how you move through life.

Self-esteem is often confused with confidence, but they are not the same thing. Confidence is how capable you feel in a particular moment or task. Self-esteem is broader and deeper; it is how worthy you feel as a person. Confidence can rise and fall with circumstances. You might feel confident giving a presentation, but unsure in a social setting. Self-esteem is more constant. It is the steady sense that you are enough, that your value does not depend on performance, perfection, or comparison. When self-esteem is strong, you can face challenges without losing your sense of self. When it is fragile, even small setbacks can feel like proof that you have failed as a person.

Psychologists often describe self-esteem as the combination of two beliefs: the belief that you are capable, and the belief that you are worthy of love and respect. If one of these beliefs weakens, the whole structure begins to wobble. A person who feels capable but unworthy may achieve great things and still feel empty. A person who feels loved but incapable may hesitate to act or take chances. Healthy self-esteem balances both. It allows you to see your strengths without inflating them, and your flaws without letting them define you.

The way self-esteem forms is complex. It begins early, shaped by the way others respond to us. Children learn who they are through the mirror of their caregivers' eyes. When a parent listens, encourages, and shows affection, the child learns that they are valued. When a parent criticises, ignores, or withholds warmth, the child begins to question their worth. These messages sink deep, often becoming invisible scripts that play throughout adulthood. Someone who grew up feeling unseen may struggle to believe in their talents later, even when they have objective proof of success. Someone who was only praised for achievements may learn to tie their worth to constant performance, afraid to rest or fail.

But life does not end with childhood conditioning. The mind remains capable of change throughout adulthood. Every experience of respect, kindness, and achievement can slowly reshape that inner mirror. The brain learns from repetition, and self-esteem grows through consistent, intentional practice. When you choose to treat yourself with compassion, you begin to build new patterns of self-recognition.

When you keep promises to yourself, you strengthen self-trust. When you allow yourself to be imperfect without punishment, you train your mind to accept your humanity instead of fearing it.

Think of self-esteem as the soil in which every other part of your life grows. Relationships, ambitions, and happiness all take root there. If the soil is weak or neglected, nothing can thrive for long. You might find temporary satisfaction from success or affection, but it will fade if the foundation underneath remains unstable. When the soil is strong, even hard seasons do not destroy what grows within it. This is why self-esteem work is not self-indulgence; it is maintenance for the very system that sustains your wellbeing.

In today's world, that mirror of self-perception is under constant pressure. Every time you scroll through social media, you encounter images of other people's highlight reels, their achievements, their vacations, and their confidence. Without noticing, you begin to measure yourself against those snapshots, forgetting that they are edited fragments of someone else's life. The more you compare, the more distorted your reflection becomes. What was once a private sense of worth turns into a public scoreboard. This is one of the costs of modern living: our sense of self becomes outsourced to other people's reactions.

To rebuild or strengthen self-esteem in such an environment, it helps to reclaim ownership of your reflection. This means deciding which voices you allow to influence how you see yourself. It means questioning the standards that have been handed to you, about beauty, success, intelligence, or happiness, and asking whether they truly serve you. It means recognising that worth cannot be proven through likes, grades, or promotions, because it does not reside in them. It resides in your character, your choices, and the integrity with which you live.

Healthy self-esteem does not blind you to your faults; it allows you to confront them without shame. It does not demand constant positivity; it invites honesty without cruelty. It does not make you self-absorbed; it helps you see yourself clearly enough to stop needing constant reassurance. In practical terms, building self-esteem often begins with small acts of internal correction. When you catch yourself thinking, "I always mess things up," you can reframe it as, "This didn't go as planned, but I can learn from it." When you notice yourself shrinking from opportunity because of fear, you can remind yourself that courage is not the absence of fear but the willingness to act despite it.

One useful way to visualise self-esteem is through what psychologists call the "self-concept wheel." Imagine a circle divided into several parts: physical self, social self, emotional self, and ideal self. Each part contributes to your overall sense of identity. When one area dominates, for example, when physical appearance overshadows emotional or intellectual worth, balance is lost. Reflecting on this wheel can help you identify which areas need more attention. Perhaps you invest heavily in work but neglect relationships. Perhaps you care deeply for others but struggle to extend the same care to yourself. The goal is to bring each area into harmony so that no single definition of self carries all the weight.

As you move through this book, you will see that self-esteem is not a fixed trait to be measured or graded. It is an ongoing relationship, one that requires awareness, patience, and regular care. It deepens each time you forgive yourself, each time you speak truthfully, and each time you choose growth over self-judgment. It is not built in a single moment of inspiration but through many small, steady acts of self-respect.

Take a moment to consider this: how do you speak to yourself when no one else can hear you? That inner tone reveals more about your self-esteem than any outer achievement ever could. The path to confidence and peace begins not with a new title or validation but with a single decision, to see yourself as worthy of kindness, both from others and from within.

ꕤ

2

WHY SELF-ESTEEM MATTERS

There are moments in life when everything seems to depend on what you believe about yourself. The interview you walk into, the exam you prepare for, the relationship you choose to stay in or leave, all of these depend less on external circumstances and more on the certainty, or uncertainty, you hold within. Self-esteem is the silent compass that guides you through those decisions. It does not announce itself loudly, but its presence or absence changes everything about how you approach the world.

High self-esteem is not arrogance, nor is it blind optimism. It is a balanced awareness of your value, combined with the courage to act on it. It allows you to walk into a challenge without needing to be perfect and to face rejection without seeing it as a reflection of your entire worth. It gives you the steadiness to persist when things go wrong and the humility to keep learning even when things go right. People with strong self-esteem are not those who never doubt themselves;

they are those who recover from doubt quickly because they have built trust in their own ability to cope.

When your self-esteem is high, you begin to interpret life differently. A mistake becomes feedback, not failure. Criticism becomes a chance to grow, not a reason to shrink. Success becomes a form of expression, not validation. You stop viewing life as a constant test and start seeing it as a process of evolution. This shift is transformative because it changes how your nervous system and mind react to everyday experiences. Instead of bracing against the world, you start moving with it.

The psychological benefits of strong self-esteem ripple through every part of your being. Emotionally, it creates stability. People who like and respect themselves tend to experience less anxiety because they no longer treat every setback as a personal verdict. Mentally, it increases focus. When you are not busy second-guessing your worth, you have more cognitive energy to direct toward meaningful work. Physically, it even affects health. Studies have shown that chronic low self-esteem is linked to higher stress hormones, weaker immunity, and sleep difficulties, because the body mirrors the mind's tension. Strengthening self-esteem is therefore not just an emotional exercise; it is a holistic form of self-care.

In relationships, high self-esteem changes the dynamics entirely. When you value yourself, you stop tolerating what harms you. You no longer chase validation from others because you have found stability within. You are able to love freely without fear of rejection and to receive love without suspicion. A person with strong self-esteem can disagree without hostility and apologise without humiliation, because their worth is not threatened by imperfection. They do not need to dominate others to feel strong or diminish themselves to feel accepted. Their confidence is grounded and contagious.

In professional life, self-esteem often separates those who survive from those who thrive. The difference between two equally skilled people often lies in self-belief. One may hesitate, doubt, or overanalyse opportunities, while the other takes initiative, learns quickly from failure, and keeps moving forward. This is not a matter of talent but of trust, trust in one's ability to adapt, to grow, and to find solutions. People with higher self-esteem tend to set clearer goals, seek constructive feedback, and handle criticism with perspective rather than defensiveness. Their resilience does not come from never falling, but from the confidence that they can rise again.

Low self-esteem, on the other hand, drains potential. It makes people question every decision, dismiss compliments, and sabotage progress before it begins. They may feel undeserving of success or love, so they unconsciously create conditions that confirm their beliefs. Over time, this becomes a cycle that reinforces itself. Every missed opportunity or failed attempt deepens the sense of inadequacy, and every attempt to escape it feels heavier than the last. This is why it is so important to address self-esteem at its core rather than trying to mask it with achievements or appearances. Real confidence cannot be borrowed from success; it must be built from self-respect.

Consider how differently people behave when they believe in their values. A student who trusts their ability to learn studies with curiosity rather than fear. A professional who feels competent takes risks that lead to innovation. A parent who respects themselves models emotional strength for their children. In every case, self-esteem becomes a multiplier, amplifying effort into results. It does not guarantee a smooth path, but it ensures that even detours lead somewhere meaningful.

To build high self-esteem, one must learn to separate worth from outcome. You can fail at a project and still remain capable. You can make mistakes and still remain good. You can be criticised and still remain worthy of respect. This separation is the foundation of lasting confidence. It allows you to act with integrity, because your actions are no longer motivated by the need to prove yourself, but by the desire to grow and contribute.

Self-esteem also shapes how you treat others. People who feel good about themselves tend to extend that goodwill outward. They are less likely to compete destructively or judge harshly because they do not need to elevate themselves by comparison. They celebrate others' achievements instead of feeling diminished by them. They listen more deeply because their ego does not need to dominate every space. High self-esteem is therefore not only personal power; it is social grace. It creates kindness that does not depend on weakness or guilt, but on understanding that everyone benefits when we rise together.

It is also worth acknowledging that high self-esteem does not mean unshakable confidence at all times. Life has seasons, and even the most grounded person will have moments of doubt or exhaustion. What distinguishes healthy self-esteem is recovery, the ability to remind yourself of your strengths after a setback, to return to balance after criticism, and to find value even in disappointment. This flexibility is what psychologists call "self-compassion in motion," and it is the mark of emotional maturity.

Developing such steadiness is not about constant affirmation or forced positivity. It is about cultivating self-trust through consistent action. Each time you show up, keep a promise, complete a task, or speak honestly, you prove to yourself that you can rely on yourself. Over time, that reliability becomes confidence. You begin to believe that even if things fall apart, you will not. That is real strength, not the absence of fear, but the presence of faith in your ability to rebuild.

In the end, self-esteem determines the quality of your inner life. It is the difference between living reactively and living intentionally. It shapes the thoughts that greet you in the morning and the tone with which you speak to yourself at night. It colours how you interpret every experience. And because of that, building it is not optional; it is essential. When you strengthen your self-esteem, you do not just improve your self-image. You change the way you participate in the world. You walk with a sense of grounded purpose, knowing that no matter what happens around you, you are enough as you are.

ജ്ജ

3

THE MODERN TRAPS

Modern life is filled with extraordinary opportunities for connection, creativity, and visibility, yet it is also filled with more psychological traps than any previous generation has had to navigate. We live in a world where comparison is not occasional but continuous, where the highlight reels of others stream across our screens from the moment we wake up to the moment we fall asleep. In earlier decades, people compared themselves with neighbours or classmates. Today, we compare ourselves with millions of strangers, influencers, celebrities, and curated digital identities. This constant flood of images can silently convince even the strongest minds that they are behind in life, not good enough, or somehow lacking. It is an erosion of self-esteem that happens over time, one scroll at a time, until your inner voice stops sounding like your own and begins to sound like the silent judgment of the online world.

Perfectionism grows in this environment. Everywhere you look, someone seems more successful, more attractive, more talented, or more accomplished. The problem is not admiration. The problem is the belief that you must match or exceed these unrealistic standards to deserve acceptance or respect. Many people begin to measure their worth not by who they are but by what they can produce, display, or prove. They start believing that their value is conditional, something that must be earned over and over again. The pressure of constant performance eventually becomes exhausting. You start asking yourself impossible questions. Am I working hard enough? Am I successful enough? Am I attractive enough? These questions have no finish line, no point where you can finally relax and say you have done well. Perfectionism traps you in a cycle where nothing feels good enough, including yourself.

Social media adds another layer of complexity by creating worlds where validation is visible. Every like, comment, view, or share becomes a tiny signal that influences how people feel about themselves. For some, these digital markers feel harmless. For others, they become emotional currency. When validation is high, they feel confident. When it is low, they feel invisible. Without realising it, many begin to outsource their self-worth to a scrolling audience. The danger in this is not the platform itself but the way it trains the mind to seek approval rather than authenticity. Over time, people lose touch with their real strengths because they are too focused on what will be accepted, admired, or applauded.

There is also a trap that affects almost everyone: the illusion of effortless success. Social media rarely shows struggle, failure, confusion, or the long hours behind achievement. It shows only the results. When you see the final product without the process, it is easy to believe that others glide through life while you alone struggle. This misunderstanding creates a painful sense of personal inadequacy. You begin to assume that if something is hard for you, you must be doing something wrong. In truth, every human life contains difficulty, and every achievement contains hours of unseen effort. Realising this can soften the harshness with which you judge yourself.

Another trap of the digital age is the constant exposure to information that overwhelms the mind. The human brain was not built to process thousands of opinions, news updates, warnings, trends, and expectations in a single day. The overload creates anxiety, confusion, distraction, and a sense of being lost in the noise. When the mind is constantly overstimulated, it becomes harder to think clearly or feel grounded. Over time, this can make your inner world feel blurry and unstable, and self-esteem begins to weaken because clarity about oneself requires reflection, not constant input.

These modern traps are not signs that something is wrong with you. There are signs that you are a human being living in a highly stimulating and competitive time. The goal is not to avoid the modern world but to develop awareness and resilience within it. Start by recognising when comparison is taking over your thoughts. Pause when you feel perfectionism tightening around you like a rope. Notice when your mood shifts because of something you saw online. When you catch these moments early, you regain power. You remember that the online world is a curated environment, not a mirror of reality. You remember that your worth is not determined by numbers on a screen. You remember that growth is slow, messy, and deeply human.

You can create boundaries that protect your mind. Limit the time you spend scrolling. Choose accounts that inspire rather than discourage. Practise being present in your own life rather than constantly observing the lives of others. Strengthen the inner voice that tells you you are enough. Cultivate activities that remind you of your abilities, your values, and your individuality. These practices do not disconnect you from the modern world. They help you live in it with strength and clarity.

Most importantly, remind yourself that comparison is not a measure of worth, perfection is not the goal, and external validation is not the source of identity. The more you step back from the traps of the digital age, the more clearly you will see yourself. And the clearer you see yourself, the stronger your self-esteem becomes.

4

THE PATH TO EMPOWERMENT

Empowerment begins in the places of the mind long before it shows up in visible changes. For many people, the biggest obstacle to confidence is not the outside world but the voice inside their own head. This voice often becomes shaped by years of criticism, comparison, fear, and internalised beliefs from childhood, school, relationships, or society. Over time, it transforms into a constant commentator that tells you who you are and what you deserve. When that voice becomes harsh, unforgiving, or dismissive, it becomes difficult to grow. You can take all the right steps externally, but if your inner voice continues to undermine you, confidence cannot flourish. Rebuilding this inner voice is not simply positive thinking. It is a deep process of unlearning, relearning, and strengthening the psychological foundation that allows self-esteem to rise naturally.

The inner critic often begins as a protective mechanism. Its purpose is to prevent mistakes, prepare us for danger, and help us fit in. However, when it becomes too dominant, it can turn into a source of constant pressure and self-punishment. Many people do not notice how often this voice speaks. They do not notice how quickly they call themselves stupid for a small error or how easily they dismiss their own achievements as luck. They do not realise how deeply they have come to believe that they are not enough. Empowerment begins with awareness. It means pausing long enough to hear the tone of your inner dialogue and really observing how you treat yourself when no one is listening. Only when you become aware of these patterns can you begin to change them.

Rebuilding your inner voice requires compassion, which is not softness or indulgence but clarity and balance. Self-compassion is the ability to treat yourself with the same understanding that you naturally extend to others. It is the recognition that mistakes are part of being human, that emotions deserve space, and that growth requires patience. Many people confuse self-compassion with weakness. In reality, it is one of the strongest tools you can develop. A compassionate mind does not collapse under difficulty. It steadies itself, reflects, and then chooses a healthier response. Compassion does not let you avoid responsibility. It helps you approach responsibility without shame and without the fear of failure that keeps so many people stuck.

Another essential part of empowerment is learning to separate your identity from your experiences. Many people carry labels they picked up through painful moments. A failure becomes an identity. A rejection becomes a truth. A bad relationship becomes proof that they are unlovable. To rebuild self-esteem, you must challenge these internalised identities. You must remind yourself that a negative event is not a definition but a moment. You must learn to see experiences as chapters rather than permanent descriptions of who you are. When you create this separation, something inside you begins to open. You allow space for change by accepting that you are not fixed, but evolving.

Empowerment also grows when you start giving yourself permission to take up space in your own life. Many people have learned to silence their needs, minimise their feelings, or apologise for simply existing. They push themselves aside in order to keep the peace, avoid judgment, or maintain relationships. Over time, this self-silencing becomes a habit and then a belief. The first step toward empowerment is reclaiming your right to matter. This means acknowledging your needs without guilt and allowing your emotions to have a legitimate place in your life. It means recognising that your desires are as valid as anyone else's and that wanting something for yourself does not make you selfish. This mindset does not create arrogance. It creates balance.

A supportive inner voice also requires boundaries, because empowerment is not just about how you speak to yourself. It is also about how you allow others to speak to you. When your boundaries are weak, your self-esteem becomes fragile because any criticism, disrespect, or manipulation can penetrate easily. Strong boundaries do not mean shutting people out. They mean choosing the conditions under which you allow relationships to shape your self-worth. Boundaries protect your emotional space so that your inner voice can grow without being constantly bruised by the outside world.

Rebuilding self-esteem also means recognising your own courage. Many people overlook their resilience because they are used to surviving difficulties. They forget the strength it took to rebuild after a loss, or the patience they showed while supporting someone else, or the discipline required to continue working even when they were exhausted. When you take time to acknowledge your own strength, and privately, you reinforce the belief that you are capable. Empowerment grows not only from new achievements but also from recognising the resilience that already exists within you.

As you rebuild your inner voice, you will also need to develop a new relationship with failure. Failure is not an insult to your worth but a teacher that helps refine your path. People with strong self-esteem are not those who never experience failure. They are people who interpret failure differently. Instead of seeing it as a verdict, they see it as information. This shift is powerful. It allows you to stay persistent and curious instead of collapsing into shame. It also encourages you to take chances, learn new skills, and explore unfamiliar opportunities without the constant fear of doing something wrong.

Empowerment becomes stronger when you replace self-criticism with self-support. This does not mean ignoring your flaws or pretending everything is fine. It means guiding yourself with fairness instead of hostility. A supportive inner voice says, You made a mistake, but you can correct it. You feel anxious, but you are capable of trying. You struggled today, but tomorrow is another chance. This voice is not unrealistic. It is balanced, patient, and grounded in the understanding that growth takes time.

Over time, as the inner voice grows stronger, you begin to move through life differently. You make decisions with more clarity. You navigate relationships with less fear. You set goals without assuming you will fail. You begin to feel steadier in your own skin. This is the essence of empowerment: a deep internal stability that does not depend on external approval. The empowered mind does not need perfection. It simply needs truth, patience, and the willingness to believe that you are worthy of becoming who you want to be.

ꕥ

5

RELATIONSHIPS AND SELF-ESTEEM

Relationships are one of the most powerful mirrors we have. They reflect how we feel about ourselves, what we believe we deserve, and how we respond to love, conflict, and connection. From early childhood to adulthood, the people around us help shape our sense of identity. Their words and actions leave marks on how we see our worth. Healthy relationships can strengthen self-esteem by offering support, understanding, and encouragement. Unhealthy relationships can weaken self-esteem through criticism, disrespect, or emotional neglect. Because of this, the quality of your relationships often becomes one of the clearest indicators of how you value yourself.

Many people do not realise how closely self-esteem and relationships are linked. Someone with a strong sense of worth tends to choose relationships that honour their needs, respect their boundaries, and allow them to grow. They gravitate toward people who treat them with kindness because they believe kindness is what they deserve. Someone with fragile self-esteem, however, may tolerate behaviour that hurts them. They may cling to relationships that drain them or tolerate disrespect because they fear being alone or believe they are unworthy of better treatment. Without noticing it, they begin to build environments that reinforce their insecurities rather than heal them.

This is why understanding your relationship patterns is essential for building confidence. Every relationship, whether romantic or platonic, influences your inner world. If you find yourself constantly giving more than you receive, always apologising for things that are not your fault, or silencing your needs to keep the peace, these patterns are signals. They reveal not only dynamics within the relationship but also how you have learned to treat yourself. When you ignore your feelings or minimise your value to maintain harmony, you unintentionally teach your mind that your voice matters less. Over time, this weakens your self-esteem because it reinforces the belief that you must shrink in order to be loved.

Healthy relationships do the opposite. They invite you to be fully present without hiding your emotions or pretending to be someone you are not. When you have people around you who listen without judgment, who speak to you with respect, and who support your growth, it becomes easier to believe that you are worthy of love and belonging. Healthy relationships do not eliminate conflict. They simply create an environment where conflict does not define your worth. They also allow you to express discomfort, set boundaries, and communicate honestly without fear of being punished or abandoned. These experiences strengthen your sense of self and deepen your trust in your own identity.

Partnerships in adulthood often highlight self-esteem more intensely than any other area of life. Romantic relationships can bring out deep insecurities because they require vulnerability, emotional honesty, and trust. People with low self-esteem may worry about being abandoned and may read too much into minor disagreements. They may feel threatened by their partner's independence or success, believing that they are not enough. They may also overcompensate by becoming overly accommodating, trying to earn love rather than receiving it naturally. This pattern often leads to exhaustion, resentment, or emotional imbalance.

To build a healthy relationship, you must first examine what you believe love should feel like. If you grew up in an environment where love was unpredictable, conditional, or tied to achievement, you may subconsciously expect relationships to involve tension or emotional strain. If acceptance is scarce, you may think you need to prove your worth to be loved. Empowering yourself in relationships begins by recognising these early impressions and rewriting them. Healthy love feels steady, respectful, and safe. It does not demand perfection or punish vulnerability. It grows best in an environment where two people feel valued, not judged.

Boundaries are also crucial to maintaining self-esteem in relationships. A boundary is not a wall. It is a line that lets others know how you wish to be treated and what you will not accept. Boundaries protect your emotional health and prevent your identity from being overshadowed by someone else's needs or expectations. When you set boundaries, you affirm your right to comfort, respect, and safety. People with strong self-esteem set boundaries naturally because they understand their own worth. People with weak self-esteem often fear that boundaries will upset others or cause rejection. However, the opposite is true. Boundaries create clarity, reduce resentment, and build trust. They are a sign of maturity and emotional strength.

Friendships also play a significant role in shaping self-esteem. A supportive friend can become a source of encouragement and honesty. They remind you of your strengths when you forget them. They challenge your self-doubt and bring humour into moments of stress. However, friendships can also become draining if they involve constant comparison, judgment, or emotional imbalance. A friend who consistently belittles your achievements or dismisses your feelings can cause damage to your self-image. Healthy friendships allow you to grow without fear of being overshadowed or misunderstood. They create a space where you feel included and accepted as you are.

Relationships within families can be equally complex. For many people, early family dynamics form the blueprint for how they behave in adult relationships. Patterns like people-pleasing, emotional withdrawal, or avoiding conflict often begin in childhood. When family members are supportive and emotionally available, children often grow into adults who feel secure and confident. When families were unpredictable or critical, children may grow into adults who struggle with trust, self-worth, or assertiveness. Rebuilding self-esteem sometimes requires examining these origins with honesty and compassion. It is not about placing blame. It is about understanding the roots of your reactions so you can make healthier choices moving forward.

Finally, empowerment in relationships grows through communication. When you express your needs honestly and listen openly to others, relationships become more balanced. Many conflicts in relationships are not caused by a lack of love but by a lack of clarity. Communicating does not mean arguing. It means expressing your inner experience respectfully and giving others the chance to respond. The more you communicate, the more confident you become in your ability to maintain healthy bonds. And the stronger your sense of self becomes, the easier it is to build relationships that support and elevate your well-being.

Healthy relationships and strong self-esteem reinforce each other. When you build one, you strengthen the other. As you learn to value yourself, you naturally begin to choose relationships that reflect that value. And as you surround yourself with people who honour your worth, your inner confidence grows steadily. This is the cycle of empowerment. It begins within you but expands outward into every connection you form.

ꟸ

6

PARENTING AND SELF-ESTEEM

A child's sense of self-worth begins forming long before they understand the meaning of the word self-esteem. It develops in the background, shaped by every interaction, every tone of voice, every moment a parent chooses to listen or dismiss, comfort or criticise, encourage or ignore. Children do not learn self-esteem through definitions. They learn it through experience. They absorb their value from what the significant adults in their lives reflect back to them. When a parent responds with warmth, attention, and respect, the child internalises the belief that they deserve to be seen and heard. When responses are cold, inconsistent, or dismissive, the child begins to question their worth long before they learn to speak about it.

The foundational years of childhood are powerful because children interpret the world in emotional terms. They are constantly asking, without words, a silent question: am I safe and am I loved? The way parents answer this question through their behaviour shapes how children interpret every challenge that comes their way. A child who grows up feeling emotionally safe learns to try new things, take risks, and recover from mistakes because they trust that their value is not determined by a single outcome. A child who grows up feeling criticised, compared, or controlled learns to fear mistakes, retreat from challenges, or please others at the expense of their own voice. These early patterns often follow them into adolescence and adulthood.

Parents often underestimate how easily children absorb their emotional environment. A child may not understand adult problems, but they can sense tension, exhaustion, or disinterest. When parents are overwhelmed, distant, or inconsistent, children sometimes internalise the idea that they must earn love by performing well, behaving perfectly, or meeting unrealistic expectations. Others may go in the opposite direction and stop trying altogether because they feel they can never succeed enough to be valued. Healthy self-esteem grows when children learn that they are loved not for what they achieve but for who they are. This unconditional sense of worth becomes the foundation on which all future confidence is built.

The way parents communicate becomes one of the clearest indicators of the environment they create. Children thrive when communication is patient, warm, and respectful. They grow anxious when communication is abrupt, unpredictable, or harsh. Even small gestures, such as making eye contact when a child speaks or acknowledging their feelings without judgment, strengthen their sense of identity. When a child hears comments like you always do this wrong, why can't you be more like your sibling, or I don't have the time for this right now, they internalise these moments as reflections of their worth. Parents do not need to be perfect, but they do need to be aware that tone and consistency matter far more than they realise.

Parents also shape self-esteem by modelling behaviour. Children do not simply listen to what a parent says. They observe how a parent treats themselves. A child who watches a parent constantly criticise their own appearance, dismiss their abilities, or doubt their value begins to believe that insecurity is normal. A child who observes a parent offering compassion to themselves, acknowledging mistakes without shame, or speaking confidently about their abilities learns that self-respect is part of everyday life. Parenting is not only about guiding children. It is also about demonstrating the kind of inner life you hope they will build.

Some parents worry that encouraging self-esteem will make children entitled or overly confident. In reality, the opposite is true. Children who feel secure in their worth are less likely to act out, compare themselves, or seek validation through unhealthy behaviours. They handle frustration better, form healthier friendships, and develop stronger problem-solving skills because they trust themselves. Entitlement grows when affection is used as a reward rather than a constant. True self-esteem grows when children feel loved consistently and understand that limitations, boundaries, and structure exist not to restrict them but to support their growth.

It is also important for parents to recognise the role of repair. Every parent makes mistakes. There will be days of impatience, raised voices, or misjudgments. The key is not perfection but recovery. When a parent apologises to a child, it teaches the child that relationships can heal and that mistakes are not a source of shame. A parent who says I am sorry for how I spoke earlier or I understand I hurt your feelings and I want to listen models humility and emotional maturity.

This helps children learn that conflict does not diminish love and that resolving it is an act of strength.

As children grow, parents must gradually shift from guiding to supporting. Young children need constant reassurance and structure, but as they age, they need autonomy, respect, and the opportunity to make choices. A child whose every decision is controlled may grow into an adult who struggles with independence or fears failure. A child who is given space to explore, make small mistakes, and discover their preferences grows into an adult who trusts their own judgment. Supporting autonomy means listening more attentively, allowing children to solve problems on their own, and recognising that developing confidence requires letting go at the right times.

Modern parenting also requires navigating influences that previous generations never faced. Social media, hyper-competition in academics, and the pressure to perform publicly add layers of complexity to a child's developing self-esteem. Parents who remain emotionally present, who create opportunities for offline connection, and who teach children how to think critically about what they see online offer a powerful shield against these pressures. Open conversations about comparison, perfection, and authenticity help children understand that what they see on screens is not a measure of their worth. A grounded, attentive parent becomes a child's anchor in a world of shifting expectations.

The foundation years set the tone for a child's lifelong relationship with themselves. When parents create environments of safety, respect, and unconditional love, children grow into adults who carry those qualities forward. When parents nurture emotional strength, communicate with intention, and model compassion, they help shape a generation that knows how to stand tall without stepping on others and how to value themselves without questioning their right to exist. Parenting is not only about raising children. It is also about shaping future adults who understand their worth deeply and carry that understanding with confidence.

ꕥ

7

ENCOURAGING GROWTH

Confidence in childhood is not built in dramatic, life-changing moments. It grows through small, repeated experiences that teach children they are capable, valued, and safe. Every time a child is encouraged to try something new, every time their effort is acknowledged, and every time they are given space to explore, a layer of self-belief forms. When parents learn to recognise these daily opportunities and use them intentionally, they help children build the kind of inner strength that lasts far beyond childhood.

Children develop confidence through doing. They learn who they are by testing their abilities, observing the world, experimenting with ideas, and making mistakes. When adults make space for exploration, children discover resilience through action. A child who struggles with a puzzle and finally succeeds experiences a deep sense of personal capability. A child who climbs a small height or solves a simple problem without help receives not just accomplishment but a powerful message: you can rely on yourself. Confidence grows when adults step back enough to allow genuine effort, while remaining close enough to provide emotional safety. Balancing encouragement with gentle detachment gives children room to grow.

Much of a child's confidence comes from how adults respond to their attempts rather than their outcomes. When parents rush in to correct mistakes, fix problems, or complete tasks for children, they unintentionally signal that the child is incapable. When parents allow children to struggle within safe boundaries and acknowledge the effort involved, the child learns endurance, creativity, and self-trust. It is not about letting children fail without support, but about helping them understand that failure is not a reflection of their worth. It is simply part of learning. A child who is taught to see mistakes as stepping stones becomes a teenager and an adult who is not afraid to try.

Language plays an enormous role in shaping confidence. Children hear their parents' words long before they understand their intentions. Praise is powerful, but it must be meaningful. When praise highlights effort rather than perfection, children learn to value the process of growth. Telling a child that you worked hard on that or that I saw how long you stayed focused teaches them that their actions matter, not just the final result. In contrast, attaching praise only to outcomes can make children fearful of trying new things because they worry about disappointing others. Confidence grows through encouragement that recognises authenticity, persistence, and curiosity.

Play is one of the most underrated tools for building self-esteem. During play, children experiment with cooperation, imagination, leadership, problem-solving, and emotional expression. It is a natural space where children learn mastery without pressure. When adults engage in play with openness and presence, they communicate that the child's interests and inner world matter. When adults allow children unstructured time to play independently, they give them room to think, invent, and test their abilities. Every tower built, drawing created, or game invented helps children experience themselves as capable and resourceful individuals.

Another important component of confidence is trust. Children flourish when they feel trusted by the adults around them. Trust communicates belief. When a parent allows a child to choose their outfit, pour their own drink, or participate in family decisions appropriate to their age, the child internalises the message that their thoughts and actions have value. Trust must be offered gradually and with sensitivity to each child's readiness, but when it is done consistently, it nurtures a sense of personal agency. A trusted child becomes a confident teenager who is better equipped to make decisions rather than simply follow instructions.

Parents can also nurture confidence through emotional validation. When children are told that their feelings are unreasonable, dramatic, or inconvenient, they begin to doubt themselves. When feelings are acknowledged gently and without judgment, children learn that their emotional experiences are legitimate. A child who hears it is understandable that you feel upset right now learns to trust their inner world. This trust becomes the foundation for self-respect. Teaching children how to name their feelings, reflect on them, and express them appropriately strengthens their sense of identity and prepares them for emotional regulation later in life.

Creating routines that encourage responsibility also builds confidence. When children are given age-appropriate tasks within the home, such as arranging their school supplies, feeding a pet, or helping set the table, they begin to see themselves as contributors to the family system. Contribution creates belonging, and belonging is vital for self-worth. When tasks are framed as meaningful and achievable, children feel proud of their ability to help, and this pride strengthens their confidence.

Children also need moments of healthy challenge. Too much protection blocks growth, but too much pressure overwhelms it. The goal is to present opportunities that are slightly above the child's current comfort zone. These gentle challenges teach children that they can stretch beyond what feels familiar. Whether it is trying a new activity, speaking in front of a small group, or learning to apologise after a mistake, each small challenge builds resilience. Confidence grows each time a child realises that they can survive discomfort and emerge stronger.

Parents and caregivers may find it helpful to integrate simple practices into daily life that reinforce a child's sense of worth. These do not require elaborate planning. Sometimes the most powerful gestures are the simplest. Making time each day for a short one-on-one conversation, showing genuine interest in the child's stories, or acknowledging small victories can create a nurturing emotional atmosphere. Regular rituals, such as bedtime reflections or weekly family check-ins, provide predictable spaces where children can share openly and feel heard.

For added clarity and application, here are a few practical prompts that integrate naturally into daily routines without interrupting the reflective flow of parenting:

Simple Confidence-Building Prompts for Daily Life

- Ask your child what they felt proud of today and listen without evaluation.
- Invite them to teach you something they learned or discovered.
- Offer choices in small matters to strengthen their decision-making.
- Point out moments where they showed kindness, effort, or creativity.
- Allow safe mistakes and talk through what they learned from the experience.

These prompts gently reinforce a child's inner strength, offering them a sense of ownership over their growth while reminding them that they are seen, valued, and capable.

Confidence in children does not grow through grand gestures. It grows through the steady presence of adults who believe in them, guide them with patience, and give them space to evolve. It grows through warm words, open conversations, consistent boundaries, and opportunities to try. The more children experience themselves through these supportive interactions, the more they build the enduring confidence that follows them into every stage of life.

༺༻

8

THE TEENAGE MIRROR

Adolescence is a time when everything feels louder and sharper. Emotions intensify, friendships take on new significance, and the search for identity becomes an urgent inner mission. Teenagers begin to look outward for cues about who they are, while simultaneously trying to pull away from the influences that shaped their childhood. It is an age of exploration, vulnerability, and tremendous potential. At the heart of this stage lies a fragile and rapidly evolving sense of self-esteem. Teenagers are building the inner scaffolding of their adult identity, and during this period, the way they see themselves can shift dramatically from one day to the next.

The teenage mind is constantly balancing two opposing forces. On one side is the desire to stand out and be recognised as unique. On the other hand is the deep longing to fit in and avoid the sting of exclusion. Belonging becomes a central psychological need, and teenagers often feel pressure to adjust their behaviour, appearance, or opinions to secure approval. This pressure can lead them to abandon their natural interests or silence their authentic voice just to blend into a group. When belonging becomes tied to performance or conformity, a teenager's self-worth can erode. They begin to measure themselves not by who they are but by how well they match the expectations around them.

The digital world intensifies this tension. Teenagers today grow up in an environment where comparison is constant and instant. Every scroll exposes them to filtered beauty, curated achievements, and exaggerated lifestyles. Their brains, still developing the ability to regulate emotion and assess reality, are especially vulnerable to believing the illusions they consume. Social media can become a hall of mirrors where they rarely see themselves reflected accurately. Likes and comments may feel like currency, and the fear of missing out can shape every decision. When self-esteem becomes tethered to online validation, the emotional costs can be significant. Teenagers may struggle with anxiety, withdrawal, perfectionism, or an unstable sense of identity.

School also becomes a landscape of rising expectations. Academic performance, extracurricular success, and future planning often pile onto a teenager's shoulders at the very moment when they feel least sure of themselves. Many teenagers interpret their struggles as personal weaknesses rather than natural parts of growth. A disappointing test score or a conflict with a friend can feel like a reflection of their worth. Without guidance, they may start to internalise a harsh story about who they are. When this happens, their confidence begins to shrink long before their adults notice the signs.

This is why teenagers need environments where they feel safe to express uncertainty. They need adults who can tolerate their shifting opinions, intense emotions, and growing independence without interpreting these changes as rebellion. When parents create a space where teenagers can speak honestly without fear of judgment, they protect their child's developing identity. Teenagers are far more willing to listen to advice when they feel heard first. A conversation in the car, a shared task at home, or a late-night check-in can become powerful bridges to connection. When adults respond with curiosity rather than criticism, teenagers learn that their inner world matters and that their worth remains intact even when their behaviour fluctuates.

Teenagers also need guidance in interpreting the pressures they face. Adults can help them understand that comparison rarely reveals the full truth and that perfection is not the standard for a meaningful life. Conversation becomes a tool for grounding. Asking questions like what made today feel difficult or what part of that situation felt overwhelming encourages teenagers to explore their emotional experiences more deeply. This process helps them recognise the difference between external pressure and internal value. Over time, they learn that their worth does not have to rise and fall with every grade, comment, or social interaction.

Peer relationships also shape teenage self-esteem. Friendships become a central source of identity, and the quality of these relationships often determines whether a teenager feels supported or isolated. Healthy friendships teach mutual respect, trust, empathy, and emotional boundaries. Unhealthy ones create confusion, dependency, or self-doubt. When adults talk openly about the qualities of healthy relationships and gently point out troubling patterns, they give teenagers the vocabulary to describe their experiences. Encouraging them to reflect on how they feel around certain people can help them differentiate between friendships that nourish them and those that drain them.

To make this chapter more practical without breaking its reflective flow, here are a few integrated prompts and examples that can help teenagers navigate this complex stage of life:

Ways to Support Teenagers in Building Healthy Self-Esteem

- Invite them to share their stories rather than interrogate them about behaviour.
- Encourage offline hobbies that build competence, such as music, sports, art, or volunteering.
- Talk openly about social media illusions and how curated images can distort reality.
- Help them set small, achievable goals to rebuild confidence after setbacks.
- Praise their decisions and values rather than their appearance or performance.
- Encourage them to choose friendships based on how they feel, not how they appear to others.

Teenagers thrive when they feel seen in their struggle. Every moment of understanding, patience, and genuine interest contributes to a stable sense of identity. They begin to trust that they can grow without having everything figured out immediately. When teenagers know they are valued for their character, not their performance, their confidence becomes steadier and more resilient. This inner stability is what allows them to take healthy risks, form deeper relationships, and face the challenges of adulthood with greater strength.

What teenagers need most is reassurance that they do not have to perfect themselves to belong. They need reminders that growth is messy, identities evolve, and mistakes are simply part of becoming. When adults provide consistent guidance and unconditional support, teenagers learn to see themselves with kinder eyes. And when they learn to treat themselves with kindness, they begin to develop the confident, grounded self-esteem that will steady them through the years ahead.

ຣ໑ය

9

ADULT SELF-ESTEEM

Adulthood brings freedom, independence, and a sense of personal agency, but it also introduces a different kind of pressure. The world begins to measure you by what you produce, what you earn, how quickly you advance, and how well you juggle responsibilities that never seem to pause. Many adults carry an invisible weight that grows heavier over time, not because they are incapable, but because the rhythm of modern life constantly asks them to be more. As expectations rise and comparisons become harder to escape, self-esteem often becomes the first casualty. Adults may not speak about it openly, yet the struggle to feel worthy enough shapes their choices, relationships, and emotional well-being in profound ways.

The workplace is one of the most significant arenas where this battle plays out. Careers can either build confidence or slowly erode it. A promotion can make someone feel capable, recognised, and seen, while a period of stagnation can create doubts that spread far beyond job performance. Many adults internalise workplace stress as a reflection of their identity rather than a challenge that lives outside them. When goals are missed or deadlines slip, they interpret the setback as a flaw instead of a moment of learning. In environments where competition is intense and success is publicly measured, the inner critic can grow loud, persistent, and unforgiving. It often takes deliberate effort to remind oneself that worth is not determined by a job title or the pace of achievement.

Rejection is another powerful force that shapes adult self-esteem. Whether it is a failed interview, a project that falls flat, a strained friendship, or the end of a relationship, rejection can cut deeply because adults carry layers of earlier disappointments. These past wounds often resurface at moments of stress, making setbacks feel heavier than they actually are. People begin to question their abilities or their likability, even when the situation says nothing about their inherent worth. Self-esteem weakens when adults forget that rejection is part of life, not an indictment of character. Healing begins when they learn to separate their identity from external outcomes and view rejection as a step in growth rather than a verdict on who they are.

The modern world adds unique pressures that past generations did not face in the same intensity. Adults today live in a culture of constant visibility, where achievements are shared instantly and compared endlessly. Social media creates a stage where everyone appears to be succeeding at once. Friends buy homes, travel, get promoted, and achieve milestones that seem out of reach. Even though logic tells us that these are curated glimpses and not full realities, the emotional impact is still powerful. The mind does not always calculate the difference between online illusions and lived truth. Without conscious effort, comparison becomes a daily habit, and over time, it begins to warp the sense of self. Adults start to judge their progress by someone else's timeline rather than by their own values and desires.

Financial pressure also plays a significant role in adult self-esteem. It is difficult to feel confident when resources are stretched thin or long-term goals feel distant. Many adults attach their self-worth to income, savings, or material accomplishments, believing these markers define adulthood. When financial goals are delayed or disrupted, they often feel embarrassed or inadequate, even though economic circumstances are influenced by countless factors beyond personal control. A healthier form of self-esteem comes from learning to define success internally rather than externally. It grows when people recognise the courage it takes to keep going, to adapt, and to make thoughtful decisions even under pressure.

Relationships in adulthood introduce their own complexities. Romantic partnerships can either strengthen self-esteem or expose its vulnerabilities. A loving relationship can help someone feel respected, valued, and understood, but even healthy relationships require emotional maturity and a stable sense of self-worth. When adults rely too heavily on their partners to validate them, they risk creating dependency. When they doubt their own value, misunderstandings and insecurity often follow. Building a strong sense of identity becomes essential for forming relationships that are balanced and nurturing. Friendships also shift during adulthood, often shaped by changing priorities, distance, or lifestyle differences. Many adults silently experience loneliness even while surrounded by people. The lack of meaningful connection can trigger self-doubt, leading some to assume they are the problem, when in truth they are simply in a stage of transition that requires patience and active effort.

One of the most overlooked challenges adults face is the grief of unmet expectations. Many people carry dreams from childhood or early adulthood that remain unrealised. These unfulfilled plans can weigh heavily, often resurfacing during moments of reflection. A person may wonder if they took a wrong turn or if they are running out of time. This can create a sense of urgency that distorts self-esteem, making adults believe they have fallen behind. It is important to recognise that timelines are human inventions, not universal truths. Growth can happen at any age, and many achievements arrive later in life precisely because experience, clarity, and resilience take time to develop.

Despite these pressures, adulthood also provides powerful opportunities for rebuilding self-esteem. Adults have the capacity to reflect deeply, make intentional choices, and shape their lives from a place of awareness rather than impulse. They can identify the beliefs they inherited and decide whether those beliefs still serve them. They can question the stories they tell themselves about failure, identity, and worth. They can build healthier boundaries, choose more supportive environments, and invest in relationships that nurture growth. Every intentional action, no matter how small, becomes a brick in the foundation of stronger self-esteem.

To add gentle structure and practical value without breaking the reflective flow, here are a few integrated tools that adults can use to strengthen their sense of worth:

Practical Ways Adults Can Rebuild Self-Esteem

- Set achievement-independent goals such as learning a new skill or completing a personal project purely for its emotional reward.
- Replace comparison with curiosity by asking what genuinely matters to you instead of measuring yourself against others.
- Create a small circle of people who offer truth, support, and perspective during moments of doubt.
- Practice self-reflection at the end of the week by noting three decisions you are proud of, regardless of outcome.
- Challenge self-critical thoughts by asking whether they come from past experiences rather than present truth.
- Redefine progress as consistency rather than speed, focusing on steady effort instead of dramatic results.

As adults learn to apply these ideas, they begin to untangle their worth from the noise of competition and expectation. Confidence grows from the inside out, shaped by self-respect, resilience, and a willingness to honour one's own journey. With time, adults discover that they do not need perfection to feel worthy. They need presence, patience, and the courage to believe in their value even when the world feels demanding. When this inner strength begins to surface, adulthood becomes not a test of endurance but a chance to create a life that feels meaningful, grounded, and fully one's own.

10

HEALING FROM THE INSIDE OUT

Healing begins the moment a person decides that their past no longer gets to define their future. For many people, low self-esteem is not a sudden development but the slow accumulation of moments that chipped away at their sense of worth. Childhood comments that were meant as jokes, academic struggles that felt like personal failures, relationships that bruised the heart, or environments where affection had to be earned rather than given all leave marks unconditionally. These marks may seem small at first, but they shape how a person sees themselves long after the moment has passed. Healing requires the willingness to finally turn toward these memories, not with blame or resentment, but with understanding, patience, and a gentle readiness to grow.

Past wounds often settle into the mind in ways. A child who was constantly compared to others often grows into an adult who questions every success and doubts every ability. Someone who received affection only when they performed well may enter adulthood believing that love is conditional. A person who experienced neglect might struggle to trust that others will stay. These patterns are not weaknesses. They are survival strategies formed at a time when the person did not have many choices. The mind learned to protect itself in the best way it could with the tools it had. As adults, people can finally begin to choose new tools. They can question the old stories and rewrite their understanding of themselves.

Shame is one of the heaviest emotions that grows out of past experiences. While guilt says, "I made a mistake," shame insists, "I am the mistake." This belief corrodes confidence and creates a barrier between the person and their potential. Shame does not always come from dramatic events. Sometimes it grows from years of feeling unseen or unvalued. Sometimes it comes from being told, directly or indirectly, that one is too much or not enough. Healing from shame involves challenging the voice that says you are unworthy and replacing it with a kinder, more truthful perspective. It requires stepping back and asking whether the criticism you internalised was ever truly about you or more reflective of what others were going through at the time.

One of the difficulties in healing is that the past often reappears in the form of present behaviour. People may repeat patterns without realising the connection to earlier experiences. They may seek out familiar dynamics, even painful ones, because they feel comfortable or predictable. They might silence themselves in conversations, avoid opportunities, or stay in unhealthy relationships because the emotional script feels familiar. Recognising these patterns is often the first step toward breaking them. When people begin to observe their own reactions with curiosity instead of judgment, they create the mental space needed for genuine transformation.

Forgiveness becomes an important part of healing, but it is often misunderstood. Forgiving does not mean excusing harmful behaviour or pretending the pain did not matter. It means releasing the emotional grip that the past has on the present. It means letting go of the idea that your worth is defined by how others treated you. Forgiveness is not a gift to the person who caused the harm, but a gift to yourself. It softens the emotional residue that weighs you down and clears the path toward a future shaped by intention rather than injury.

Healing also involves giving yourself what you did not receive in earlier years. If you grew up without encouragement, you may need to learn how to speak to yourself with kindness and support. If you lack emotional security, you may need to practice self-soothing and build internal stability. If you often feel invisible, you may need to learn how to take up space in your own life and allow yourself to be seen. This process is not quick, but it is transformative. With consistency, self-compassion becomes a natural instinct rather than an unfamiliar effort.

Because healing requires both emotional and practical steps, it can help to incorporate a few grounded tools into daily life without disrupting the flow of reflection. These tools act as small anchors that bring clarity and direction while the deeper emotional work unfolds:

Helpful Practices for Healing Past Wounds

- Begin a gentle reflection practice where you write about past experiences, not to relive them but to understand how they shaped your beliefs.

- Practice speaking to yourself the way you wish someone had spoken to you when you were younger.
- Identify one old pattern you want to release and one new pattern you want to strengthen. Focus on consistency rather than perfection.
- Surround yourself with people who respect your growth, especially during vulnerable moments when self-doubt is loud.
- Create physical or emotional boundaries that protect your energy and signal to yourself that your well-being matters.
- Develop a grounding routine, such as walking, reading, mindful breathing, or listening to music that brings calm, to help regulate emotions during difficult memories.

Healing from past wounds also means learning to see your story with more compassion. Every struggle you faced required resilience. Every disappointment taught you to adapt. Every setback carries a lesson that helps shape who you are today. Many people reach adulthood believing they are broken, when in truth they are simply carrying unprocessed hurt. Once they start to understand their history through a kinder lens, they begin to see that they are not failures but survivors who learned to endure. This shift in perspective often marks the beginning of deep emotional renewal.

As healing continues, people often discover that the past loses its sharpness. The memories remain, but they no longer dictate the narrative. Confidence grows because it is no longer built on fragile foundations. People become less reactive, less anxious, and less apologetic for who they are. Their relationships become healthier because they choose from a place of self-worth rather than fear. Their goals become clearer because they are no longer trying to prove their value to others but pursuing what genuinely matters to them.

Healing is not a straight path. It bends, loops, and sometimes slows, but it always moves if you stay present and patient. With time, the emotional weight begins to lift. In its place comes a steadiness, the kind that does not need constant validation and does not crumble under pressure. This steadiness becomes the true sign of healed self-esteem, the inner assurance that you deserve peace, respect, and joy. When the past no longer whispers doubts into the future, you finally feel free to build a life that reflects your true worth.

ꟙ

11

THE POWER OF AFFIRMATION AND APPRECIATION

Words shape the way we see ourselves more than most people realise. A single sentence spoken at the right time can strengthen belief, inspire courage, or soothe a tired spirit. A careless remark, even one dropped casually in frustration, can linger for years and influence how a person evaluates their worth. Because language has this extraordinary power, the words we speak to others and the words we speak to ourselves often form the emotional architecture of our lives. When we begin to understand the impact of this internal and external dialogue, we also begin to understand why affirmation and appreciation hold such transformative potential.

Affirmation is not simply the practice of repeating positive statements. At its heart, it is the process of re-learning how to speak to yourself with honesty, encouragement, and dignity. Many people grow into adulthood carrying the echoes of critical voices from their early years. These echoes shape their inner dialogue, and without noticing it, they begin addressing themselves in the same dismissive way they once heard from others. Breaking this pattern begins with awareness. When you pause long enough to listen to your own thoughts, you may discover that your mind has been speaking to you in a tone you would never use with someone you love. Affirmations help shift this tone by creating a new internal language that supports growth rather than undermining it.

The most effective affirmations are those that feel meaningful rather than forced. A statement like "I am worthy of respect" only becomes powerful when you repeat it with intention and allow it to settle into your understanding of yourself. Over time, such statements soften the grip of old beliefs and open space for confidence to grow. Affirmations work gradually, shaping self-perception through repetition and emotional engagement. They help interrupt the old cycle of criticism and replace it with a kinder voice that feels more truthful and grounded.

Appreciation is just as essential, although it expresses itself differently. While affirmations focus on how you speak to yourself, appreciation highlights what you observe, acknowledge, and value in your own actions. Many people move through their days so quickly that they forget to notice the small successes that reflect their strength. They overlook their patience in difficult conversations, their effort during stressful situations, or the discipline it took to make a healthy choice. As a result, they come to believe they are not doing enough, even when they are demonstrating resilience every day. Appreciation helps correct this imbalance by bringing attention to the qualities that already exist within you and deserve recognition.

One of the most profound aspects of appreciation is that it does not require dramatic victories. In fact, it is most powerful when applied to the small, consistent actions that often go unnoticed. When you take a moment to acknowledge that you handled a conflict with grace or completed a task despite feeling tired or resisted the urge to fall back into an unhealthy habit, you reinforce the belief that you are capable and growing. This internal acknowledgement creates momentum. You begin to trust yourself more. You begin to see yourself not as someone who is constantly falling short, but as someone who is evolving and capable of handling life with increasing confidence.

Because both affirmation and appreciation rely on habits of awareness, they benefit from simple daily practices that help integrate them into everyday life without disrupting the reflective flow of the chapter. These practices are gentle and adaptable. You do not need to follow them perfectly for them to work. What matters is consistency and sincerity.

Practices for Strengthening Affirmation and Appreciation

- Spend a few minutes each morning speaking to yourself the way you would speak to a loved one who is trying their best.
- Identify one belief that has held you back and create a truthful, compassionate affirmation that challenges it.
- At the end of the day, write down three moments, however small, where you acted in alignment with who you want to become.
- Notice when your self-talk becomes harsh and pause long enough to shift it to something more grounded and encouraging.

- Acknowledge emotional effort with the same seriousness you give physical or professional effort. Inner work deserves recognition, too.

Affirmation and appreciation also have a powerful effect on relationships. When you speak kindly to yourself, you naturally begin to speak more kindly to others. When you appreciate your own progress, you become more generous in appreciating the efforts of those around you. People who practice consistent appreciation tend to create environments of emotional safety, where others feel comfortable being themselves. These environments strengthen connection and deepen trust because appreciation validates effort, and validation makes people feel seen. In this way, the practice of speaking kindly to yourself is never limited to your internal world. It radiates outward and influences the emotional tone of your home, your friendships, and your partnerships.

It is also important to recognise that affirmation does not mean pretending everything is perfect. It simply means choosing to speak to yourself with hope rather than defeat. Appreciation does not mean ignoring areas that need improvement. It means balancing self-awareness with gentleness so that growth can happen without shame. Self-esteem thrives in environments where honesty is paired with compassion. Affirmation and appreciation work together to create exactly that environment. They strengthen identity without inflating ego, and they encourage effort without creating pressure.

Over time, the combination of these practices builds a deeper sense of self-respect. You begin to see your strengths clearly and accept your imperfections without judgment. You no longer depend on external validation to feel worthy, because your internal foundation becomes stronger. This stable confidence becomes the mark of someone who has healed from past criticism and is learning to speak to themselves with the dignity they always deserved.

The true power of affirmation and appreciation lies in their simplicity. They ask only that you notice your worth and speak to yourself with care. When practised consistently, these small shifts in language can reshape your entire relationship with yourself. They create a mindset where confidence can grow naturally. They nurture resilience by reminding you that you are capable of facing whatever challenges arise. And they bring a sense of emotional steadiness that allows you to walk through life with a renewed sense of worth.

ജ്ജ

12

TOOLS FOR GROWTH

Lasting self-esteem does not grow by accident. It is cultivated through a combination of self-awareness, guidance, and experience, and it strengthens most effectively when a person chooses to learn from multiple sources rather than relying on one single path. In the modern world, we have more tools for growth than any generation before us. Therapy is more widely available, self-help literature is abundant, online communities can offer support, and seminars and workshops provide spaces where learning becomes experiential. Each of these tools has a distinct role in shaping how we understand ourselves, yet they all point toward one simple truth: everyone has the capacity to learn, to heal, and to rebuild the inner foundation that gives rise to healthy self-worth.

Therapy is one of the most powerful tools for rebuilding self-esteem because it allows you to see yourself more clearly. Many people carry stories from their childhood or early adulthood that they have never fully examined. These stories may involve criticism they internalised, relationships that shaped their self-image, or failures they interpreted as proof of their inadequacy. When left unexamined, these experiences settle into a person's belief system and influence their behaviour long after the moment has passed. Therapy creates a safe space where these narratives can finally be explored without fear or defensiveness. A good therapist helps you separate the truth of who you are from the distorted ideas you once believed out of necessity or habit. Through this process, self-esteem begins to rise not through fantasy but through clarity, because you finally see the difference between what happened to you and who you truly are.

Many people hesitate to seek therapy because they assume it is a sign of weakness, but the truth is that it is a sign of courage. It takes strength to sit with your emotions, to admit that something feels difficult, and to take steps toward change. Therapy teaches emotional literacy, which is the ability to recognise, name, and respond to emotions with understanding instead of fear or avoidance. When you build emotional literacy, you become less controlled by your reactions and more in touch with your deeper needs. This clarity strengthens self-respect and makes it easier to navigate relationships because you begin to understand where your boundaries should be and how to uphold them without guilt.

Seminars and workshops offer a different kind of growth experience. While therapy focuses on deep introspection, seminars often focus on active learning, practical skills, and shared human experience. A good seminar can remind you that you are not alone, that others struggle with similar fears, and that growth becomes easier when it is shared. There is something uniquely transformative about being in a room filled with people who are also learning to value themselves. The collective energy creates a sense of encouragement that is difficult to replicate alone. You begin to feel part of something larger, part of a community of human beings who are learning, failing, healing, and trying again. This belonging can itself become a powerful source of confidence because isolation is one of the forces that weakens self-esteem, while connection naturally strengthens it.

Self-help practices form the third pillar in this chapter, and they often act as the everyday stitching that holds the broader work together. These practices can include journaling, meditation, mindfulness, guided reflection, reading, or structured exercises that help you track and understand your thoughts. Self-help practices work because they bring consistency into the growth process. A weekly therapy session may give you direction, but it is the daily self-practice that deepens the insight and makes it part of your behaviour. Journaling, for example, helps you see patterns that are hard to recognise in the moment. Over time, you begin to notice that certain thoughts appear when you are tired, stressed, or overwhelmed, while other thoughts appear when you are hopeful or grounded. This awareness allows you to catch early signs of emotional decline and respond with healthier tools rather than falling into old habits.

Mindfulness is another self-help practice that has tremendous power. It teaches you how to stay present, how to watch your thoughts without being consumed by them, and how to recognise the difference between who you are and what you feel in a moment of difficulty. When mindfulness becomes a natural part of your life, self-esteem no longer rises and falls with every challenge. Instead, you develop a steady inner anchoring that allows you to hold yourself gently even during moments of insecurity. Mindfulness also builds patience, and patience is one of the strengths of people with high self-esteem because they understand that progress unfolds over time rather than in dramatic leaps.

Although this chapter emphasises therapy, seminars, and self-help practices, it is important to remember that none of these tools replace the internal work of honesty. Growth does not happen simply because you attend a workshop or complete a few exercises. It happens because you are willing to look at yourself fully, including the parts that feel tender or uncomfortable. These tools provide structure, guidance, and support, but the effort must come from within. When you combine external support with internal intention, you create a powerful foundation for lasting transformation.

It can also be valuable to blend these tools rather than choosing only one. Many people find that therapy helps them explore their past, seminars help them build skills for the future, and self-help practices help them stay focused in the present. When these approaches work together, growth becomes multidimensional. You heal old wounds, build new strengths, and practice daily habits that deepen your self-trust. You begin to feel more aligned with yourself and less dependent on external validation because your confidence grows from the inside.

To help integrate these tools in a simple and practical way, you may want to consider a gentle weekly structure that gives space for each kind of growth without overwhelming you. For example, you might reserve one day a week for deep reflection or therapy, another day for learning through books, videos, or seminars, and a few minutes each evening for mindfulness or journaling. Such a structure offers balance. You learn from others, you learn from professionals, and you learn from yourself. Over time, you begin to see that self-esteem is not built through occasional breakthroughs but through small, consistent investments in your well-being.

The true value of these tools lies in how they help you relate to yourself. When used consistently, they teach you how to understand your fears without being ruled by them. They remind you that healing is possible at any age. They help you discover strengths you thought you had lost. They give you language for emotions you once struggled to explain. They teach you how to care for your mind with the same seriousness you give to physical health. And perhaps most importantly, they give you the clarity to recognise your own worth, even on the days when you feel unsure of yourself.

Self-esteem flourishes when knowledge, support, and consistent practice come together. Therapy provides insight, seminars provide inspiration, and self-help practices provide momentum. When you allow these tools to support your growth, you begin to build a sense of self that is solid, compassionate, and deeply rooted. You realise that your worth was never something you had to earn. It was something you had to uncover. These tools simply help you remember what has been true all along.

ꕥ

13

YOUR SELF-ESTEEM ACTION PLAN

Rebuilding self-esteem is not a single decision but a commitment you make to yourself day after day. It is a gradual unfolding, much like sunlight easing across the sky at dawn. The shift is real, but it happens gently, steadily, layer by layer. Many people believe confidence is something you either have or do not have, but in truth, confidence grows in the same way a muscle grows. It grows through use, through gentle repetition, through consistent attention, and through moments of discomfort that lead to strength. The purpose of this action plan is not to provide rigid rules but to give you a structure that supports your transformation. You are not building a new version of yourself. You are uncovering the version that has always been there beneath the noise, the pressure, and the self-doubt.

A good action plan begins with clarity, and clarity begins with honest awareness. Before you can build higher self-esteem, you need to understand the patterns that have shaped your current beliefs. Spend time each day noticing how you speak to yourself. Notice the tone, the words, the assumptions. Most people are far harsher toward themselves than they would ever be toward someone they love. They dismiss their accomplishments, magnify their flaws, and forget their strengths. An action plan for healthy self-esteem begins with interrupting this habit. Even a small shift in self-talk changes the inner atmosphere. When you gently replace criticism with curiosity, you create space for growth. Instead of asking what is wrong with you, ask what you need. Instead of asking why you cannot do something, ask how you can begin.

It is also important to bring structure into your daily life. Self-esteem falters when life feels chaotic or overwhelming, because uncertainty feeds anxiety and doubt. A simple daily routine helps create psychological safety. It tells your mind that you are capable of taking care of yourself. You might begin each day with a short moment of intention, setting a tone for how you want to feel or behave. This does not need to be elaborate. A sentence like "Today I choose patience" or "Today I choose to honour my needs" can anchor your mindset throughout the day. Even on difficult mornings, having a gentle intention reminds you that you are not powerless. You are choosing your direction, not reacting to it.

Another foundation of the action plan is the practice of reflection. Reflection allows you to slow down long enough to understand your emotional landscape. Without reflection, you may repeat old patterns out of habit without understanding why they still hold power. Try spending a few minutes each evening writing about what went well, what felt difficult, and what you learned about yourself. This is not a journal of complaints but a tool for clarity. Over time, you will start to notice patterns. You will see what triggers your insecurity, what strengthens your confidence, and what types of situations invite old wounds to resurface. This awareness allows you to respond with intention rather than reacting from fear or habit. Reflection becomes a map, revealing where you have grown and where you want to focus your energy next.

As you build self-esteem, you must also cultivate small, meaningful victories. Confidence rises when you set goals that are realistic and still meaningful. Small goals have power because they prove to you that change is possible. It may be as simple as finishing a task you have been avoiding, speaking up in a meeting, setting a boundary with someone who drains your energy, or taking a moment to rest when you feel overwhelmed. Each small success builds trust in yourself. You begin to see that you are capable of following through, capable of caring for yourself, and capable of shaping your future. With time, these victories accumulate into a strong sense of inner competence.

To support these changes, consider integrating a few structured practices gently into your routine. These are not rigid steps but flexible tools you can adapt based on your personality and life circumstances.

1. **Daily grounding practice**
   Spend a few minutes each morning with a grounding activity. This may be slow breathing, a brief stretch, a walk outside, or a moment of reflection. Grounding helps regulate the nervous system and builds emotional steadiness.
2. **A weekly truth check**
   Choose one moment each week to check in with yourself honestly. Ask what has been taking your energy, what has been giving you strength, and what you need to adjust. This habit prevents emotional buildup and keeps you moving with clarity.

3. **A monthly growth review**

   At the end of each month, reflect on how your self-talk, boundaries, relationships, and habits have shifted. This long-view perspective helps you see growth you might otherwise overlook and strengthens motivation.

4. **The practice of boundary-setting**

   Boundaries are essential for healthy self-esteem. They protect your energy and identity. Practice saying no when needed. Practice communicating your needs clearly. Practice stepping back from situations that overwhelm or diminish you. With each boundary you set, your self-respect grows.

5. **The three-kindness rule**

   Commit to offering yourself three small acts of kindness each day. It might be pausing to rest instead of pushing through exhaustion, speaking to yourself with compassion during a mistake, or allowing yourself time to pursue something you enjoy. These small acts rebuild inner trust.

Alongside these practices, it can be valuable to incorporate gentle affirmations into your life. Affirmations are not meant to magically erase years of insecurity. They are meant to slowly reshape your internal narrative. Choose affirmations that feel truthful and grounding rather than overly grand. For example, "I am learning to trust myself" or "I am allowed to take up space" can be more effective than statements that feel unrealistic. Over time, these reminders begin to sink in and soften the harsh edges of your self-talk.

Another important element of the action plan is cultivating environments that support your growth. Self-esteem does not develop well in isolation or in relationships that constantly undermine your worth. Surround yourself with people who speak with kindness, who listen without judgment, and who respect your boundaries. Healthy environments reinforce healthy beliefs. You do not need a large circle of support. Even one person who sees your worth can make a significant difference. If such people are not present in your life yet, allow this chapter to remind you that you are worthy of supportive relationships and that you can create them with time and intention.

Finally, remember that rebuilding self-esteem requires patience. You are unlearning years of conditioning and replacing it with compassion and clarity. This work takes time. There will be days when old patterns return, and that does not mean you are failing. It simply means you are human. Growth happens through repetition, through reflection, through small acts of courage, and through a willingness to begin again. With each page of this journey, you have learned more about yourself, more about your needs, and more about the strength that has always lived within you.

This action plan is not a rigid checklist but a living guide. It will grow and change with you. You may adapt it based on your experiences, your age, your responsibilities, and your emotional needs. What matters is not perfection but commitment. When you choose each day to honour your worth, you take one more step toward a life rooted in confidence, clarity, and strength.

Your self-esteem will rise not because the world changes, but because you begin seeing yourself with kinder, more truthful eyes. That is the heart of this action plan, and the beginning of a life lived with deeper self-respect and authentic confidence.

CONCLUSION

There comes a moment in every journey when the path stops being about what you need to fix and starts becoming about what you choose to honour. That moment is the beginning of true self-acceptance. It arrives without ceremony. It may appear in the middle of an ordinary day, when you suddenly realise that you are no longer speaking to yourself with the same harshness as before. It may surface in the way you respond to a mistake, not with shame but with understanding. Or it may shine through in the small choices that used to feel overwhelming but now feel natural. This is the confidence you have been building throughout this book, the kind of confidence that does not shout or boast, but simply exists as a steady presence within you.

Self-acceptance is not the absence of flaws. It is the understanding that your imperfections do not diminish your worth. Many people spend years chasing perfection, believing that once they become flawless, happiness will finally arrive. But real happiness begins the moment you stop trying to become someone else and start recognising the value of who you already are. Confidence grows from this recognition. It is rooted in the decision to believe that you deserve respect, rest, care, opportunity, and love. When you accept yourself fully, you stop fighting your reflection and begin meeting it with compassion. Every part of you, even the parts you once tried to hide, becomes something you understand rather than fear.

Throughout this journey, you have explored the many forces that shape self-esteem. You have examined the influence of childhood wounds, modern pressures, social comparison, relationships, and internal narratives. You have looked honestly at the patterns that weaken your confidence and the habits that strengthen it. You have learned how self-esteem is built through deliberate practice, through reflection, through gentle correction, and through the courage to change what no longer serves you. This understanding is the foundation of self-acceptance. When you know why you think the way you do, when you understand the roots of your insecurity and the triggers that unsettle you, you become less reactive and more grounded. You start to respond to life with intention rather than fear.

Confidence does not come from achieving extraordinary things. It grows through small, consistent acts of self-respect. It grows each time you set a boundary, each time you speak honestly, each time you choose rest instead of exhaustion, each time you allow yourself to learn something new without demanding immediate perfection. Confidence develops when you make mistakes and choose to keep growing. It expands when you forgive yourself. It strengthens when you recognise how far you have come, even if the milestones seem invisible to others. Confidence is built not through dramatic changes but through steady presence. It is the kind of confidence that stays with you even on the days when things are difficult.

Self-acceptance also means understanding that your worth does not depend on your productivity, your appearance, your achievements, or the approval of others. These are external measures, and external measures shift constantly. When you rely on them for validation, your self-esteem rises and falls like a fragile flame in the wind. True confidence, however, is grounded. It remains steady because it comes from within. It comes from the belief that your existence carries meaning simply because you are human, not because you meet certain standards. When you internalise this truth, you develop a calm that protects you from the noise and pressure of the world. You learn to approach life with gentleness and strength, knowing that your value is constant.

As you move forward, there will be days when old habits return. You may hear echoes of old criticism or feel the sting of comparison again. This does not mean you have failed. It simply means you are human. Growth is not linear. It is a process of expanding and contracting, rising and resting, learning and relearning. What matters is that you keep returning to yourself. You keep choosing kindness over harshness. You keep reminding yourself that you are worthy of the same compassion you extend to others. With time, the kind voice becomes louder than the critical one. With practice, the sense of worth becomes stronger than the doubt.

The confidence of self-acceptance is not something you perform. It is something you live. It shows up in how you carry yourself, in the way you treat others, in the way you handle setbacks, and in the way you honour your own needs. It grows in your silence, your presence, your choices, and your willingness to keep becoming. The work you have done throughout these pages is not a temporary fix. It is the beginning of a lifelong relationship with yourself. One built on honesty, compassion, resilience, and patience.

As you close this book, let the final thought be simple and steady. You are worthy. Not because of what you do, but because of who you are. You do not need to earn your value. You only need to recognise it. When you live with this understanding, confidence rises naturally. You move through the world with a sense of peace and grounded strength. You learn to love yourself not in a loud or dramatic way, but in the unwavering way that lasts.

This is the confidence of self-acceptance. This is the beginning of a life lived fully and authentically. This is the truth you carry with you now and always.